The Punk Rock funTime Activity Book

by aye jay!

ECW press

Published by ECW Press
2120 Queen Street East, Suite 200, Toronto, Ontario, Canada M4E 1E2

Library and Archives Canada Cataloguing in Publication

Morano, Aye Jay
Punk rock fun time activity book / Aye Jay Morano.

ISBN 978-1-55022-872-4

1. Punk rock music—Humor. 2. Coloring books. 3. Puzzles.
4. Games. I. Title.

ML3534.M832 2009   782.421660207   C2008-907548-X

Developing editor: Jennifer Hale
Cover and text design: Aye Jay
Typesetting: Rachel Ironstone
Printing: Webcom

Cover poster artists: Arturo Vega (www.ramonesworld.com); Winston Smith (www.artcrime.com);
John Holmstrom (www.johnholmstrom.com): All images ©John Holmstrom, 2008; Mad Marc
Rude (images used courtesy Lyn Todd); Tim Kerr (www.timkerr.net), Aaron Cometbus;
Shawn Kerri; Raymond Pettibon

Exploited logo by Pushead; Ian MacKaye's hair page based on DC-area flyer by unknown; Minor
Threat bottle by Jeff Nelson; Darby photo by Jenny Lens; Circle Jerks logo by Shawn Kerri;
Nirvana photo by Michael Levine; Black Flag logo by Raymond Pettibon;
Punk Libs translations by Meka Klungtvet-Morano

Printed and Bound in Canada

ECW PRESS
ecwpress.com

Foreword: Yo Punk Rock!

by Steven Blush

Punk Rock is a state of mind. It's a self-contained universe of anger, rebellion and great music. For alienated kids it's an escape from reality. To become true Punk Rockers those kids must take deliberate giant steps away from the traditional American Way of Life. Hey, if I have to explain to you what it is, then you're not Punk!!!

The worst thing about today's mainstreaming of Punk is the way industry and media types have effectively smoothed out the edges. Punk once served a dual purpose as both a provocative musical form and a dangerous socio-political force. Now it's presented as the aural effluvia of yet another bunch of shabbily dressed Rock dudes. Anyone present back in the day remembers just how primitive, visceral, anti-intellectual and politically incorrect it all was. And as for the much-ballyhooed "unity" to which Punks are alleged to have aspired — forget it. They hated each other!

A few former members of that anti-social subculture are now considered among today's great minds. Henry Rollins offers the MTV generation PBS-flavored edu-tainment. Ian MacKaye is hailed by the same academic circles he detested as a combative teen. Jello Biafra is forever on the anti-war lecture circuit.

But the average Punk Rocker was no rocket scientist or brain surgeon. Individuals attracted to such savage sounds and scummy company weren't exactly class valedictorian material, if you catch my drift. No Punk studied classical composition, or even Led Zep guitar solos for that matter. Punk successfully articulated the need to simplify, to strip down and go back to the drawing board, to blow shit up and start again.

To that end, I'm proud to present Aye Jay!'s latest endeavor, *The Punk Rock Fun Time Activity Book*. In just 48 pages, Aye Jay! has done the impossible: dragging Punk back to the puerile, with a Crayola-friendly paperback chock fulla infantile activities like connect-the-dots, match games, coloring exercises and Mad Libs, guaranteeing hours (minutes?) of fun for children and dumb adults alike!

On the book's inside cover, Aye Jay! has assembled a murderer's row of Punk's best artists and musicians. The graphic skills of John Holmstrom and Arturo Vega, associated with *Punk* magazine and the Ramones, define the genre. Collage artist Winston Smith created the iconography for Dead Kennedys and Green Day, while the late Mad Marc Rude is synonymous with Battalion of Saints and The Misfits. Punks made intense flyers for their own bands, like Tim Kerr of the Big Boys from Austin, TX. Comic icon Jamie Hernandez (Love and Rockets) got his start doing LP cover art for Oxnard, CA, Hardcore ("Nardcore") greats like Dr. Know and Agression. Fanzine editor Aaron Cometbus is a Bay Area Punk legend.

The Punk Rock Fun Time Activity Book is a product that speaks for itself. Aye Jay!'s previous books' forewords were penned by the likes of Steve Albini and Andrew W.K., so I'm proud to be asked to represent my scene here. When I graduated from college in DC in 1984, I had no idea that 25 years later I'd still be writing about the same old crap. It's good to know that I was on the right side of the culture war!

In Rock,
Steven Blush
author/producer *American Hardcore*
NYC, 2008

FiNd THe TWO maTCHiNG SOCiaL DiSTOrTiON LOGOS

4

DRAW TATTOOS ON HENRY ROLLINS

HOW MaNY wOrdS CaN YOU make frOm SiD AND NANCY?

_____   _____

_____   _____

_____   _____

_____   _____

_____   _____

COLOR PATI SMITH

VELVET UNDERGROUND
CONNECT THE DOTS

PUNK LEGEND

Use the code to find out the name of this Tom Verlaine/Richard Hell fronted band

Code:
26=a
25=b
24=c
23=d
22=e
21=f
20=g
19=h
18=i
17=j
16=k
15=l
14=m
13=n
12=o
11=p
10=q
9=r
8=s
7=t
6=u
5=v
4=w
3=x
2=y
1=z

7　22　15　22　5　18　8　18　12　13

COLOr iggy POp

PUNK  LibS

The STOOGes
"I waNNa be YOur dOg"

So messed up I want _____ here
(pronoun)

In my _____ I want you here
(room in house)

Now we're gonna be _____-to-_____
(body part)   (body part)

And I'll lay right down in my _____ place
(adjective)

And now I wanna be your _____
(animal)

Now I wanna be your _____
(animal)

Now I wanna _____ your dog
(verb)

Well c'mon

Now I'm ready to close my _____
(body part)

And now I'm ready to close _____ mind
(pronoun)

And now I'm ready to feel _____ _____
(pronoun)   (body part/parts)

And lose my _____ on the burning sands
(body part)

And now I wanna be your _____
(animal)

And now I wanna be your _____
(animal)

Now I wanna _____ your dog
(verb)

Well c'mon

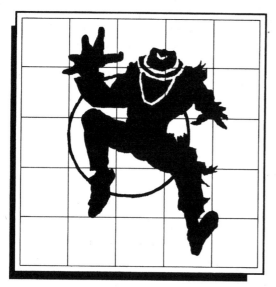

USE THE grid TO draw OPERATION IVY'S LOGO

LESTer baNGS maTch game

Match the quote to the band or artist Lester Bangs was writing about

1. "They have recorded an album up in New England that can stand, I think, easily with *Beatles '65, Life with the Lions, Blonde on Blonde,* and *Teenage Jesus and the Jerks* as one of the landmarks of rock 'n' roll history."

2. "The female role model for the '80s. Besides being one of the greatest guitarists in the world."

3. "Musically the group is intentionally crude and aggressively raw."

4. "Makes the most of the middle register while indulging a penchant for the occasional birdlike falsetto trill."

5. "They have endured more than their share of abuse, derision, critical condescension and even outright hostility."

A. MC5

B. The Stooges

C. The Shaggs

D. The Slits

E. Lydia Lunch

help The CircLe jerks' MascoT Through The mosh piT

make your own cbgb's bathroom graffiti!

Color green Day

Circle the letter of the alphabet
that matches the name of this band

A B C D E F G H I J K L M
N O P Q R S T U V W X Y Z

17

HOW MANY WORDS CAN YOU MAKE FROM MINUTEMEN?

_____   _____

_____   _____

_____   _____

_____   _____

_____   _____

_____   _____

color darby crash

LEGENDS Of PUNK WORD Search

The Adverts
Angry Samoans
The Avengers
Buzzcocks
Crime
Dead Boys
The Dicks
The Dickies
The Dictators
The Dils

Discharge
DYS
Eater
Gang Green
GBH
The Heartbreakers
The Jam
JFA
The Meatmen
The Mentors

Necros
Negative Approach
Nomeansno
Reagan Youth
Samhain
The Slits
SS Decontrol
The Stranglers
UK Subs
Weirdos

```
S S U F N Y M H W N A F R N R E Y N F G S N F A V B A W J J
P R S K H C A O R P P A E V I T A G E N R O C C F F D S J E
F Q E D S E Y K U S Z C F B H D T S M M O M G J Z R W M F Q
D I X L E U B S K H R C N E H H O Q Y M T E G P Y C P H S N
I H O P G C B C P O G S H K E D T R R P A A S Y O B D A E D
K V E O P N O S S L U E J S R H F S R O T N E M E H T P S S
G R B D S C A N I D A W L I E S U T Q C C S C M V O B B K R
K B Q M Z O G R T R K I E A Q G B Q E E I N T H E D I L S X
M U C Z B I K C T R T W D Z E Z Y S K R D O D L K H C S S B
W L U M W N S B O S O V R R M U H P P H E R B K D J T K H G
H B G G E F R O M H E L T E S V V P A Q H P Z D V Q H E F H
B R D L I E E M I R C H E E T Z U Q K S T D I S C H A R G E
T N N F A A W O T E Z P T S Y A G H I F G A I D S E L R M G
G I F K C W H S G N E V M L U F E A B K J U H L E D C Q X N
W X E P E U O M R E A G A N Y O U T H S K Y C F I C I X G C
D R Y U X Y E F G D A V L T V P N M Y D M W S T K Y Q O A F
S T Z Y M G O Z G J C V M V U B C D H T K N U H C G X Y B U
I V M X J X B X K Z G B V D V S B C C I A Y K E I P A M D R
G G Q M Q U S L G W U P Q N M U L E R O X E W A D V X Y K E
L A Y T E I U K Z I M T E Z D G R R M B X P K V E K J N T N
N V N L Q Z M W C R C J O P O P G A V I K U J E H P B I K Y
O K J G O O A O A I M S O A M V S A G B H A I N T Q H A B F
L Q Z D G W D L T F D U Q B V Y S F V W N N B G N O M H H X
T F L N W R L G Y H B E R S R X P J F C F P X E J S N M A F
O Z W N N U E P F A S Q H G P O J F R J C Y T R Y G L A C I
W Q R I Y N Z E O Z P L N T J F A O V Q O D H S A N V S Y I
Y W G G R H D I N M B A N I I I T T A N J L E I Q F R V W M
E N K M U H N E Z Z V K Z I B Z T P Q I S A J X E F S N O Q
X V E M I U V Z S E F Q W S W F S T O B Q A A T J F Y I B C
P R P D O U I S R C V N B X N F P P Y W H V M P D G C P X S
```

FINISH drawing THE SUICiDaL TENdeNCiES SKuL!

Match the quotation to the person who said it in the film

Decline Of Western Civilization

1. John Doe, X
2. Darby Crash, The Germs
3. Lee Ving, Fear
4. Greg Ginn, Black Flag

A. "It's great to be filthy rich."

B. "If I could have sex once an hour for 24 hours, I would do it."

C. "Find me a fucking beer!"

D. "When we play, they get pretty wild."

COLOR THE RAMONES

HeLP The DesceNdeNTS, miLO geT TO COLLege!

COLLege!

draw YOUrSElf aS a mEmbEr Of dEVO!

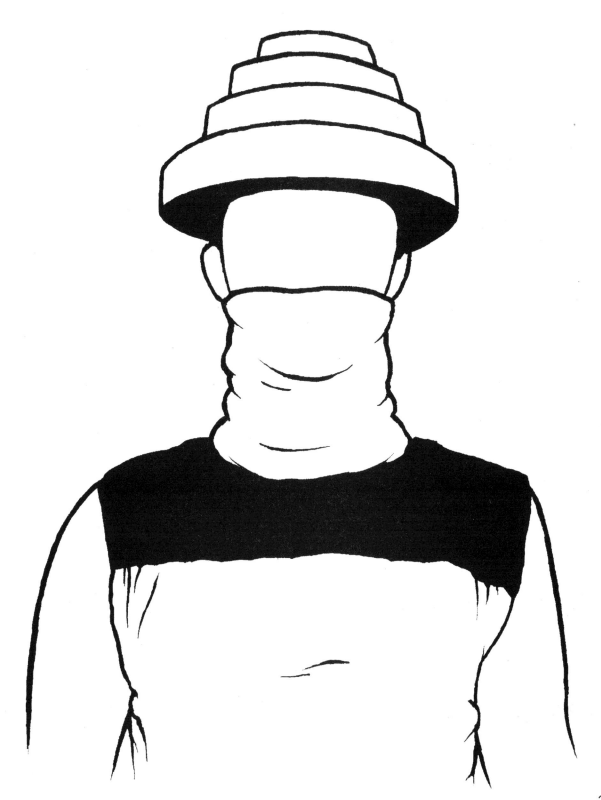

CROSSWORDS AIN'T PUNK!

Match the band to the album title below

ACROSS

4. Zen Arcade
5. The Ungovernable Force
7. Songs About Fucking
8. Kings of Punk
9. Another Kind of Blues
10. Bong Blast
16. Tell Us the Truth
17. Still Screaming
24. Sound and Fury
26. Hardcore '81
27. More Beer
28. Second Coming
29. Extinction
30. Change Today?
33. Hootenanny
34. Human = Garbage
35. Victim in Pain

DOWN

1. The Day the Country Died
2. Germ Free Adolescents
3. This Island Earth
6. Fear of a Punk Planet
10. You Axed for It!
11. Blood, Guts and Pussy
12. Queens of Noise
14. Too Much Too Soon
15. Rum, Sodomy and the Lash
18. Hairway to Steven
19. Nine Patriotic Hymns for Children
20. The Greatest Gift
21. New Hope for the Wretched
22. Inside my Brain
23. Music for Pleasure
25. Dragnet
31. Millions of Dead Cops
32. Ancient Artifacts

COLOr gg ALLiN

PUNk LEGENd

Who is this experimental two-man group from New York City?

Code:
26=a
25=b
24=c
23=d
22=e
21=f
20=g
19=h
18=i
17=j
16=k
15=l
14=m
13=n
12=o
11=p
10=q
9=r
8=s
7=t
6=u
5=v
4=w
3=x
2=y
1=z

__ __ __ __ __ __ __
8   6   18 24 18 23 22

HOW MANY WORDS CAN YOU make frOm

ADOLE-
SCENTS

_____   _____

_____   _____

_____   _____

_____   _____

_____   _____

CONNECT THE DOTS

Form the lightning bolt from the Bad Brains' album cover

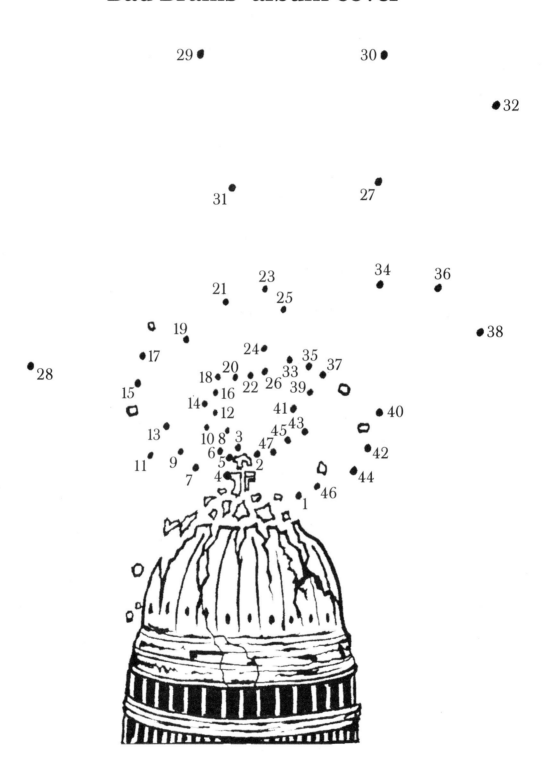

Draw The baSS guitar from The CLASh's LONdON Calling album

maTch The baNd TO iTS LOGO

1. 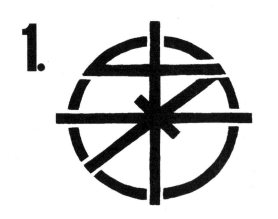   big bOYS

2.    D.R.I.

3.    fLIppEr

4.    7 SeCONdS

give ian mackaye hair

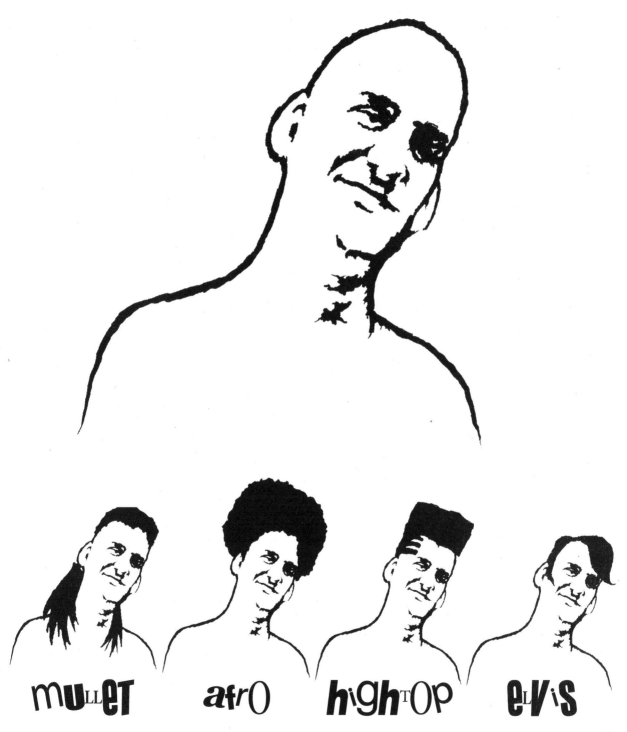

mullet   afro   hightop   elvis

COLOr NirVaNA

CONNECT THE DOTS

Draw the afro on
Rob Tyner from the MC5

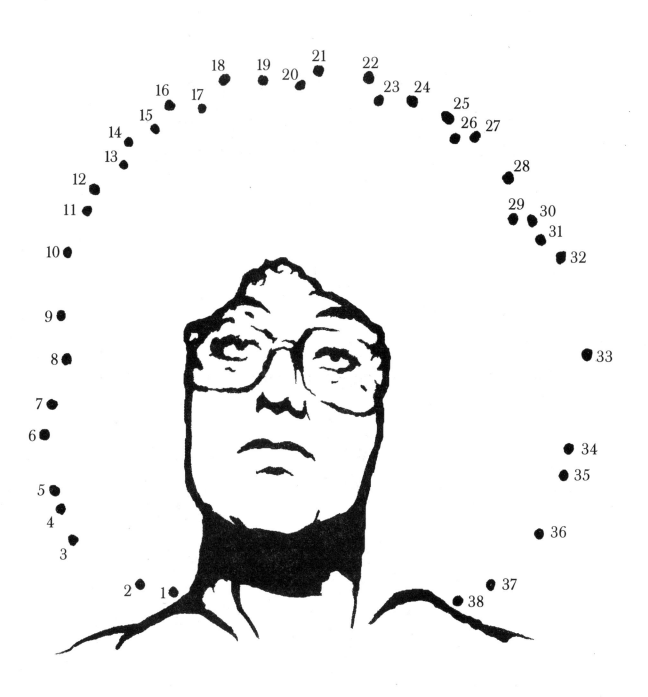

apply siouxsie sioux's makeup!

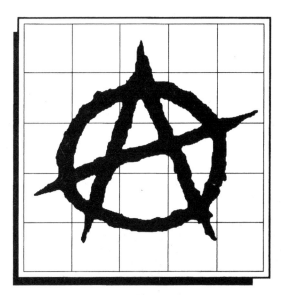

USE The grid TO draw The aNArchY SYMbOL

color jello biafra

PUNk LibS

DEad KENNEdyS' "CalifOrNia Über AllES"

I am Governor _____
(Calfornia governor)

My aura _____
(facial expression, plural)

And never _____
(different facial expression, plural)

Soon I will be _____ . . .
(elected government position)

_____'s power will soon go away
(US president, last name only)

I will be _____ one day
(another word for "leader")

I will command all of you

Your _____ will meditate in school
(noun, plural)

Your _____ will meditate in school!
(repeat previous noun)

Über Alles _____
(US state)

Über Alles _____
(repeat previous state)

California _____
(non-English expression)

California _____
(repeat previous expression)

Zen fascists will control _____
(pronoun)

_____% natural
(number)

You will _____ for the master race
(verb)

And always wear the _____ face
(emotion)

Close your _____, can't happen here
(body part)

Big Bro' on white _____ is near
(animal)

The _____ won't come back you say
(subculture/group of people)

Mellow out or you will _____
(verb)

Mellow out or you will _____!
(repeat previous verb)

39

baNd Name Scramble

Use the band logos to help unscramble the band names

1.

EDAD NKEIMLM

2.

NOMRI ARTHTE

3.

HET TASCDI

4.

SRACS

5.

CBKLA ALFG

6.

DAB IONGRLEI

HOw maNY wOrdS CaN YOu make frOm

SUB HUM ANS

_____   _____

_____   _____

_____   _____

_____   _____

_____   _____

_____   _____

FiND THE TWO MATCHiNG EXPLOiTED SKULLS

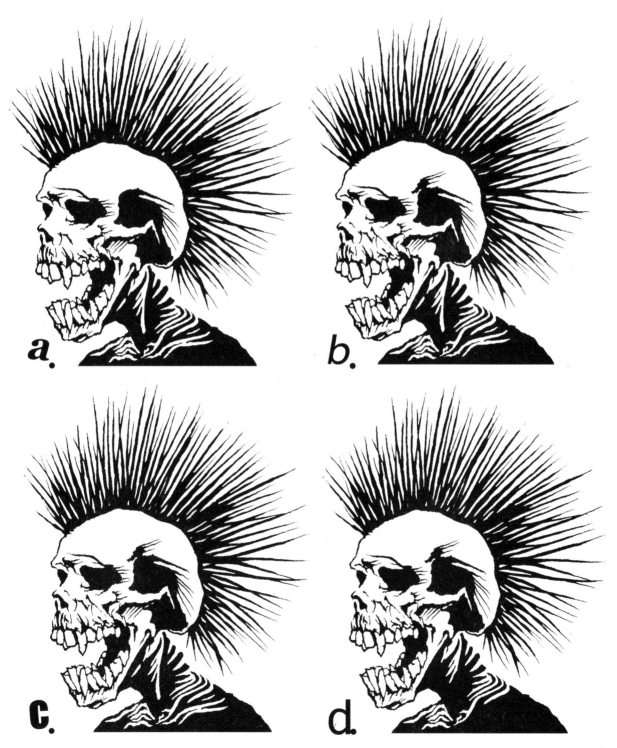

a.

b.

c.

d.

MiSfiTS PaiNT bY NUmbeRS

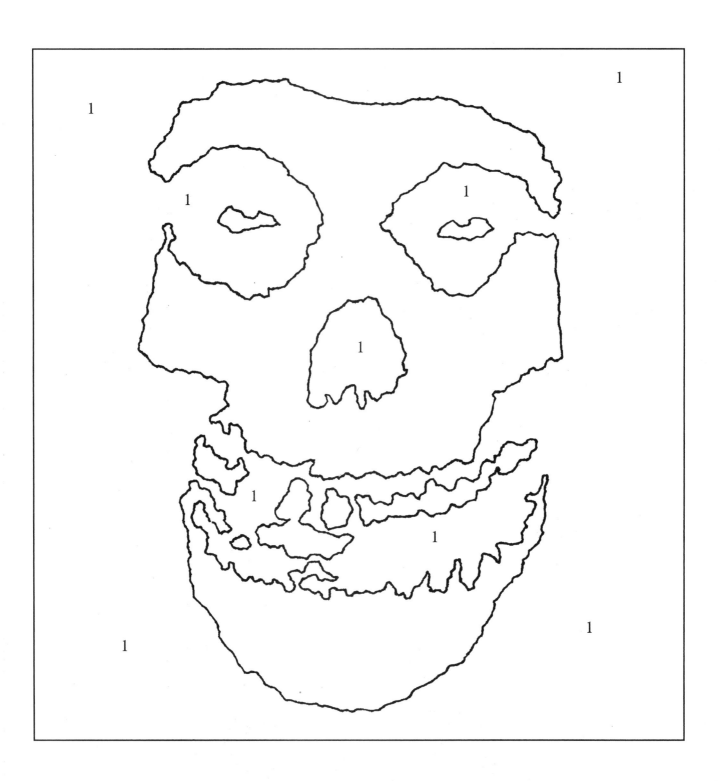

1 = black

The Cramps Song Title Word Search

Bikini Girls With Machine Guns
I Was a Teenage Werewolf
Mama Oo Pow Pow
New Kind of Kick
Zombie Dance
Goo Goo Muck
Garbage Man
Cornfed Dames
Human Fly

Journey to the Center of a Girl
Let's Get Fucked Up
Like a Bad Girl Should
Strange Love
Two Headed Sex Change
Caveman
Strychnine
Alligator Stomp
Tear It Up
TV Set

```
L G U Q F D U L K U H O M F T L U B G T B C Y I E N E H N R
M R O J B R S E L M V S P L E H E A D W B C G C N G C E F T
W Z I O D F U L E Y F T K O S Z B T S N O M N R N Q W Q C R
G G C G G J J Q E S Z R E W V K M M S N A A J A A K R N O Z
O A Z I A O W G C V F Y A E T W N G T G D M H H I P I A Y I
F H W S Y F O T T S J C O R H G K L W E E C E N J A D J H C
O L H T Y T O M J V F H S E H R U K I B X T D V H P O I I Z
D E L U O V H R U T Q N B W R K E B A E D O F H A F E J U A
A V S S Z D S E E C O I Y E B D M C S F F W F U R C I F G N
L O D Z R D T Z E T K N L G Y O J D H K J L H U C Q R R S T
L L S N F F P G F D N E P A Z G E L I Y A X Y I F K O P R P
I E E T N I Q Q E V Z E J N Y D V C H U G P C B F I E G Z M
G G U O D Z L B O P O H C E A L K H O D L C Z M T D E D O Y
A N R P F M W Y J N L I K E A B A D G I R L S H O U L D U B
T A R T V X F O J S E R H T H F O Z S D Z I Z P Y O I R R P
O R W B A I B I P Q H O V A C T J K X Y X W R M Z S B V W N
R T M I B C K Q E W W X S S X G O F N L B W L G A C U H X T
S S E N G O H Q S T O Z C A R U U T A A R N Q U S S M G O O
T B R D S G F I R V J P M W X J F P Y P U T I R A E T Q G O
O D T Y N A V U E U P P O I V A O U W E C A W V C X U M A M
M Y P J W C M O V Y F D B O J R X P N F N I G W L H T J C A
P S E M A D D E F N R O C S A F L I C G A R B A G E M A N Q
T Y V W A K S P B X N L T L N M Y K L W J V U E T J B D K H
H T T N E T G X R R E G P E H N A G Y W D M M O F R N Q U E
U N U G H D Z T O D Q F H S A F F M P N D I Y V J N G M U L
S N U G E N I H C A M H T I W S L R I G I N I K I B A O Z K
J P Q O G H O Y R R Z G K S I B N X J H E J E Q X N W R O H
K C G N Y B A O E O V H Z N C D Q H Y T S M G C F X K M S G
C L D R F F S O V Q R V P Y K B B B K U Y L M F L A K E K Q G
S U C J B X F R J J W U B R D W M O H H T M Y M B V M F V T
```

Match the Johnny Rotten Quote With its Subject

1. "He's crushing his testicles in tight trousers for world peace."

A. Joe Strummer

2. "I could take on England, but I couldn't take on one heroin user."

B. Bono

3. "They smell, big time. They're like old gorgonzola cheese in old boots."

C. CBGB's

4. "He'd already tried the pub-band circuit, so he hopped onto punk."

D. Sid Vicious

5. "That's a world of foolishness."

E. Green Day

Mad Marc Rude

A Tribute by his Wife

Mad Marc Rude is a name that has become synonymous with American punk rock and has become a pillar in The Low Brow, or underground art world. Marc's professional career began with The Misfits' Earth AD, and spanned 30 years of album covers, fliers, posters and t-shirts for so many bands that I cannot recall them all, and continued on until his death in Las Vegas on March 14, 2002.

Marc never cared much for the art world, which he found to be pretentious, superficial and downright boring. He was far too down to earth and real to sit there listening to "art lovers" discuss the nonexistent hidden meanings they saw in his work, as they sipped on their white wine and nibbled on low-fat hors d'oeuvres. He'd pull me aside and say, "I think it's pretty damned evident exactly what I am saying here. Fuck you! There are no hidden meanings; it's all right there in black and white. I'd rather have a hundred punk rock kids wearing my t-shirts and plastering my posters all over their walls than to have some rich art snob hording a piece of my work away above his fireplace so others like himself can discuss my hidden meanings and exactly what my pen strokes mean. I don't have to say a word to get my message across. I just have to do my illustrations, and my messages are heard loud, and clear, literally blasting through their skulls!"

Watching Marc work was like watching an art machine! He'd draw a line or two in pencil on the Bristol board he always worked on, and then begin with the pens, nibs and India ink. The Bristol board would begin to spin around like a turntable on amphetamines, and before you were able to realize what had happened, another piece of incredible artwork was taking form before your eyes. Marc worked at super human speeds, which was far too fast for us mere mortals to even catch a glimpse of. He'd work like a man possessed for 18 to 48 hours on each piece, never stopping until he felt it was finished. He'd say, "I do each piece as if it were my first piece and my last piece. I always put 150% into each and every piece. People come to me because they expect a certain quality of work, and the musicians that come to me work hard for the money they pay me, and they deserve the very best I can deliver, each and every time."

Throughout the many ups and downs of his life, his art remained true and straight from his heart. Marc had done and seen it all 100 times over. His life experience is reflected in his work, which was sometimes beautiful, sometimes grotesque, sometimes both, but always pure genius. His true love and salvation was his art, whether it be his illustrations or his tattoo work. Ink was in his blood. The list of bands he did artwork for is countless, and the endless amounts of work he did to promote rock 'n' roll mind boggling.

On his deathbed he dictated a letter to me which he insisted I read to his friends and fans at the inevitable memorial service. In typical Marc Rude fashion it bluntly and half-jokingly stated, "I know that all of you knuckleheads could have paid me much better for my work (you bunch of cheapskates), but I want all of you to know that I was never in it for the money! Money was never the motivation behind my work, the motivation was my deep love and respect for music . . . I never did any of it for the money. I did it all for the music, it's my contribution to rock 'n' roll."

And, what an amazing contribution it is.
— Lyn Todd-Rude

Aye Jay! Thanks:

Meka, Greta and Cohen; all artists, musicians and photographers in the book; everyone at ECW Press; Larry and Lucretia Klungtvet; the Moranos; Jean Fusco; Steven Blush; Lyn Todd; Brian Ray Turcotte (buy his books: *Fucked Up and Photocopied* and *Punk Is Dead, Punk Is Everything*); Greg Hopkins and fam; Michael Pilmer; Gerald Casale; KRK Ryden; Jeff Nelson; Ian MacKaye; Keith Morris; Henry Rollins; Jello Biafra; Jenny Lens; Blag Dahlia; Kevin Seconds; Brian Brannon; Aaron Horkey; Frank Kozik; Art Chantry; Brett Aronson and John; Glen E. Freidman; Rich Jacobs; CBGB's; Matt Loomis; Jeremy Golden; Max Flog; Patton Oswalt; Henry Owings; Paul Townsend; Gary Panter; Los Bros Hernandez; Sacha, Brent and Ego Trip; Cody Hudson; Mike 2600, Wes Winship and Burlesque Design; Kevin Boettcher; Mike Sutfin; David D'Andrea; Mike Patton; Faydog; Heathakilla; Gurp City; Ron and Colin Turner at Last Gasp; Insound; Doug Surreal; Shawna Gore; The Woot; Travis Millard and Mel Kadel; Duffy's Tavern; the City of Chico; and anyone I may have forgotten.

To the cover artists — Winston Smith, Tim Kerr, Aaron Cometbus, Arturo Vega, Shawn Kerri, Raymond Pettibon, Mad Marc Rude, John Holmstrom — you are all a huge inspiration. Thank you for your amazing work.

ANSWERS

Pg. 4, Social Distortion Match: b & c

Pg. 9: Television

Pg. 13, Lester Bangs Match:
1-c, 2-e, 3-a, 4-d, 5-b

Pg. 17: X

Pg. 22, Decline Match: 1-b, 2-c, 3-a, 4-d

Pg. 26, Crosswords Ain't Punk!:
ACROSS: 4. Husker Du, 5. Conflict, 7. Big
Black, 8. Poison Idea, 9. U.K. Subs, 10. Murphy's
Law, 16. Sham 69, 17. Scream, 24. Youth Brigade,
26. D.O.A., 27. Fear, 28. Battalion of Saints, 29.
Nausea, 30. T.S.O.L., 33. The Replacements, 34.
Dystopia, 35. Agnostic Front
DOWN: 1. Subhumans, 2. X Ray Spex, 3. Dr.
Know, 6. The Vandals, 10. Mentors, 11. The
Dwarves, 12. The Runaways, 14. New York Dolls,
15. The Pogues, 18. Butthole Surfers, 19. Born
Against, 20. Scratch Acid, 21. Plasmatics, 22.
Angry Samoans, 23. The Damned, 25. The Fall,
31. M.D.C., 32. D.I.

Pg. 28: Suicide

Pg. 32, Band Logo Match:
1-7 Seconds, 2-Flipper, 3-Big Boys, 4-D.R.I.

Pg. 40-41, Band Name Scramble:
1-Dead Milkmen, 2-Minor Threat, 3-The Adicts,
4-Crass, 5-Black Flag, 6-Bad Religion

Pg. 43, Exploited Match: b & c

Pg. 46, Johnny Rotten Quote Match:
1-b, 2-d, 3-e, 4-a, 5-c